LOVE
MUSIC

LOVE
MUSIC
And It Will
Love You Back

Essays on music by Jeff Colella

PALMETTO

PUBLISHING

Charleston, SC

www.PalmettoPublishing.com

Copyright © 2024 by Jeffrey Colella

Author Photo and Cover Design by Mikel Healey

Hardcover ISBN: 979-8-8229-3783-3

Paperback ISBN: 979-8-8229-3784-0

Preface

It is my hope that this book will prove useful to musicians and teachers of all stripes, regardless of style and regardless of respective levels of expertise and experience. It is my intent first and foremost to talk about music, how it works and what its needs are. Hopefully in these pages, musical philosophy and conception will be directly and indirectly discussed and questioned and hopefully perhaps, even inspired. After all, we do need to arrive at our own version of musical conception, and that results from our musical philosophy, does it not? Is this one of those chicken and/or egg questions? I hope not, but whichever comes first, it is the presence of both that gives birth to our musical voices. Absent our confronting these questions, we're just a collection of things learned, but not assembled and integrated into a unique musical voice. That is the goal is it not, unique musical expression? Expression that can be consistent, and musically coherent?

In the following pages I will address specific musical concepts and skills that we all have to deal with as musicians and as teachers. My ideas are born out of my many years of experience as a student, as a pianist, conductor, arranger, composer and as a teacher. I have been an improvising musician, predominantly but not exclusively a jazz pianist, all of my life. Resultantly, parts of this book address areas specific to playing, teaching and understanding jazz music and the art of musical improvisation. That being said I believe the ideas and concepts discussed here can be of use and interest regardless of stylistic inclinations.

I hope this book will provide an opportunity for us to reexamine the way we learn and teach. Music making is a complicated human endeavor, that engages and challenges the totality of our being. If there is one idea or one utterance within these pages that opens a new door for someone, or provides a new or different perspective on some aspect of making and understanding music, I will be eternally grateful.

Dedicated to Mae & Skitz
Thank you for my musical life

Table of Contents

LOVE MUSIC
AND IT WILL LOVE YOU BACK
MY THOUGHTS ON MUSIC

"When you really learn music, you learn all music.
Music is like the air and the water.
It flows from here to there,
changes its aspects,
but its essence is timeless.
It truly holds the world together."

—HERMETO PASCOAL

Like lemmings to
the sea..........

For those of us who live pretty exclusively in the world of tonal music, there is an inescapable reality. Pitch in tonal music has tendencies, places it wants or even needs to go. These tendencies are so strong and perhaps pre-dictable, that Schoenberg wanted to escape them, hence his creation of the twelve tone system of composition, an attempt to escape the gravity of tonality. By not re-peating a pitch until all 12 have sounded, pitch tendencies are mitigated if you will, there attraction to one another diminished, no established tonal center, no tonic note to run home to, pitch becomes weightless. But alas, we ton-al dwellers do in fact have tonal centers to go home to, always have had and always will have. Bach worked with them as did Bill Evans, Chopin and Brahms and Miles and Monk and Dizzy and Debussy and Ravel and Ellington and on and on and Stravinsky and Mingus and Schubert and

Porter and Gershwin and Sting, the Beatles and Dylan. All inhabitants of this tonal world we share.

There is energy in tonal relationships. Perhaps that's what draws most human beings into relationship with such music. We relate to it more naturally, are moved by it more unanimously, can hum it and remember it more easily, our ears and bodies absorb it, we are sponges for it in a way that we are not when these relationships are absent in what we hear.

So what do we do with these relationships and tendencies I speak of? How do we respond to them, feel them, hear them, shape them, play them, sing them? Compose and arrange them?

I guess the simple answer is, well, to each his or her own. We each have to explore and find our own personal relationship with and to the sounds that we make, with tonal tension and release, and movement. The beauty is that it's different for each of us, and as a result, each of us can express ourselves musically in a unique way. *Music allows us all to have our own voice.* We must allow that for ourselves, and trust that each of our musical voices is valid and worthy of expression and of making a contribution. If this wasn't so, music would have stopped long long ago. After Bach, why would Mozart even try? After Mozart why did Beethoven give it a go? After Charlie Parker why would any alto player pick up a horn? Well as we know they all did "pick up their respective horns" and aren't we profoundly grateful that they did? So music marches on, and within this finite world of tonality, of twelve pitches, musical artists have and will continue to explore their infinite possibilities.

So that is our charge, as musicians, teachers, and students, to find our way, our means of expression in music.......... our voices.

Music Moves

Music doesn't run in place, or jump up and down, or stay still..................it moves. Music, while having vertical qualities, moves horizontally. How we hear and respond to pitches moving in time from one to the next, to harmonies and their relationships one to the other and how they move in time, to and fro, has a profound influence on how we interpret and perform the music we choose to play. This relationship of pitch and harmony that I speak of, is not to be taken for granted. Music doesn't automatically happen or come to life. Playing accurately the notes we see before us on a page of written music, does not ensure that coherent, forward moving musical phrases and forms will occur. We've all heard pitch perfect performances that leave us unsatisfied, that lack a strong sense of form. And music doesn't happen automatically when we as improvisors play notes that are all theoretically sound or "correct" choices. Meaningful, intentional, communicative phrases happen when we are responding to and hearing, each in our own way, the above mentioned relationships of pitch and harmony, and their movement in time.

Importantly, this kind of hearing helps us to ask and answer the following important question; Where does this music want to go? Not where do I want to make it go, but, where is it telling me it wants to go?

There is a moment I remember as clearly as if it happened yesterday. We all have those moments that "stick", that we always remember. They are important moments. I was in a piano lesson with Dr. Guy Duckworth and our group at the University of Colorado, and I was working on a Debussy piece, and as I was playing it, Guy would say to me "let it emerge, don't force it, rather, let it emerge". As I gradually was able to understand and incorporate this concept, I began to feel as if I was hearing where and how the music wanted to go in that moment. It was a very different experience from trying to figure out or hear what I was supposed to do with the music to move it forward. It was an experience of letting it unfold of it's own free will, of letting the inherent logic of the composition play itself out. It was a different way of listening and hearing. It was like listening from "inside" the music, listening and resultantly playing from an inside-out perspective, rather than an outside-in one.

We hear great artists speak of the music "playing itself", or "the solo was there, I just let it happen, it came through me, I didn't create it so to speak, I just let it happen." These experiences are born out of the kind of listening I'm describing above. When we have this kind of experience performing I think we are hearing where the music wants and needs to go, we are inside it. Call it a musical zone if you will, a feeling that you're along for the ride, and the music is playing itself, going where it wants to go, and not being forced to go elsewhere.

Why? What? Where?

All musicians at some point in their development have to explore how they relate to sounds, to the music that they make. Why am I playing this instrument? How does this music feel to me or make me feel? What kind of music is it for me? What is my relationship to it? Where do I hear it wanting to go in this moment? What am I saying with it? What does *it* want to say?

These are not questions in search of answers that are either right or wrong. These are simply questions in search of answers, answers that we must provide every time we play music, whether we are practicing, performing, learning something new or playing something old that we've been playing for years. Music just needs these questions answered, perhaps in fact demands that we answer them, and we must answer them honestly and respectfully, time after time, day after day. That's what we do, we are musicians, we are artists.

"jazz is about closeness to the material, an intimate and personal dance with the material…"

—KEITH JARRETT

Expression

What are our expressive devices? Volume, touch, articulation, accent........grace notes, ornaments of differing kinds.........bending notes for instruments that can...... back phrasing for players and singers alike.......rhythmic alteration........melodic variation.........I'm surely missing others, but all of the above are ways of doing something to the music...........doing something that's not there in the music so to speak. So to the extent that we employ such expressive devices, we are implicitly saying that the music by itself or as it is, is lacking in some way, is absent musical life, is expressionless. What does that say about our opinion of the composers whose music we are playing? Are they that bad that what they've written is just a lifeless array of notes that would just lye there expressionless without our accents and crescendos and bends and back phrasings and all the other myriad of ways we endeavor to be expressive?

These are questions we need to answer for ourselves, questions to consider. Here are my answers: I think composers, from Bach to Beethoven to Chopin to Debussy to Stravinsky to Ellington to Monk to Porter to Rogers & Hart to Hancock to Loesser to Berlin, and we could go on and on, are quite good.........that's an understatement. I don't think their music needs us to do things to it to make it extraordinary, it already is. We need to understand it, from the inside of it, from inside to out, and *find and hear the expression that lies within.* Before we go about putting ourselves all over it, we need to hear what's there, understand its phrases and its form, the architecture of the melody, the lyrics, the tension and release of the harmony in question...............all of these elements are filled with expression just as they are. I propose that if our understanding of the music is deep and intimate, we will find our place in it. Our interpretive and expressive choices will be deeply rooted inside the music. If we approach music from the "outside", an inherently less informed place, we will find ourselves putting things on the music that don't belong. We will over use our expressive tool kit because the deeper level of musical interpretation is missing or lacking, not sufficiently informed. So in this "outside to in" case I describe, perhaps our sense as we are playing that the performance needs something more, is in fact quite correct. But, if our understanding of the music is insufficient, then we have no choice but to go to the tool box, pull out some accents and crescendos, a few grace notes, do some back phrasing and all manner of other things, but alas nothing really works. What's missing in the performance is right there in the music, we just haven't discovered it yet.

There is great beauty and expression in playing or singing great time and solid rhythms. There is great beauty and expression in a centered pitch as well. I find much too often however, we try and use time and rhythm as expressive devices, bend notes or employ grace notes unnecessarily in an attempt to be "expressive" or "musical". What happens when we do this is we often end up distorting notes in ways that are musically and expressively counter productive. We end up rushing or dragging, and our attempts at back phrasing just turn into phrases played or sung that are in fact out of time and whose rhythmic content is unintelligible. And our pitch bends and grace notes just end up obscuring what would otherwise be a beautiful melodic line.

Again, musical expression must be rooted deeply inside the music, so that our choices are motivated and organic, so they are what the music needs, and not just something we are putting on the music to dress it up because the deeper meaning it holds has eluded us.

Phrasing

Miles Davis was a master of phrasing. Whenever one speaks of the way Miles played, the word *space* is always part of the conversation. One can argue that the spaces inside of and in between phrases are as important as the notes that are played. They indeed are part of the music, and not just moments when we don't know what to say. Or perhaps another way to talk about it is to say that the silences are part of what is being said. These silences are pregnant moments, creating a tension all their own, as do fermatas and written rests in music of all styles.

Space in between utterances, be they verbal or musical, allows for time to digest what's been said, and then to formulate a response. This time to digest is necessary both for the speaker and the listener, the performer and the audience. After all, we are talking about linguistic communication, always a dialogue, a conversation, a call and response, a question and an answer, point - counterpoint.

To this point, Miles spoke of being influenced by the phrasing of Frank Sinatra and Orson Wells, one a singer, one a speaker.

Often, what I hear from beginning improvisors is run-on phrases, an almost non stop run of notes, with no distinguishable beginnings or endings of phrase. A lot of notes that go nowhere. This happens predominantly for two reasons, both fear related. One is a fear of getting lost, that if we stop playing for too long we'll lose our place in the music. So we overplay in order to keep track of where the music is, every note part of a security blanket we weave as we go. We are in no way shape or form inside the music where we should be, we're just trying to keep up with it, hang on to it. As the old saying goes "time waits for no man", well neither does music. Once the first note is sounded off the music goes and either we go with it, stay on the horse so to speak, or off we go and I assure you it won't be with the music or the horse, and a bumpy landing it will be.

The other performance fear that comes into play that impedes phrasing, is being afraid that if we stop playing for a moment, if we allow for a breath, a space, a silence, we won't hear what to say next. One has to confront this fear head on. If we don't allow ourselves space and time to hear, we'll never know what we genuinely hear or if we are able to hear something or not. We have to be able to come from a hearing place, not a thinking place. We don't want to "think" what to play next, we want to hear it. Nor do we want to come from a place of muscle memory, regurgitating a lick we learned or just playing something because our hands are in the habit of "going there" when we see a certain chord symbol or progression.

So both of these phrasing issues are fear related. On the one hand, fear we won't hear anything, i.e. we won't know what to say next, and on the other, fearing we'll get lost. Neither of these fears or anxieties are proper motivations for music making. So what's the remedy for these musical maladies? Well one thing that will certainly help is knowing the music that we are trying to play, and I mean really knowing it. So what is really knowing a piece of music?

1. Know the melody and lyrics if lyrics apply
2. Analyze and understand the form
3. Analyze and understand the harmonic structure
4. Understand the melody and phrase structure
5. Make decisions about how you are feeling the meter
6. Be able to hear the piece through from beginning to end in your head, with and without the music

The above list is a good start. I say that because I have found that as I live with the music that I play, over the course of years, I always discover something new, a different turn of phrase, a deeper understanding of form, an interpretation that I'd previously not considered, a different response to an impressionistic texture, a different harmonic possibility, a different emotional response to the music, and on and on.

Truly knowing the music we are trying to play and/or improvise on, will go a long way towards allaying our fears. In fact I think our level of fear in performance is directly proportional to our depth of understanding of the music in question. One might say that all of that is obvious, that it's a given that we need to be educated about the music we play. But alas, it seems that it's not so obvious. To the seasoned artist yes, but to students who are less experienced, and simply haven't lived long enough to have the experience of living with a piece of music for a period of years, the kind of knowing I speak of is often not yet understood. I have experienced many students who seem to think that knowing what scales to use for the chord symbols that they see is all they need to know. We as educators I think bare some responsibility or complicity in this incomplete perception of what understanding music is. I think that an over emphasis on chord scales tends to promote vertical hearing, and that puts us in a box that can be difficult to get out of.

As for being afraid we might not hear anything, we can directly confront the issue by intentionally practicing leaving space between our phrases. I'm not just talking about a beat or two, I'm talking bars, at least one at a minimum. Practicing at slower tempos is also very useful, as it helps us to break muscle memory responses and hopefully substitute them with genuine hearing responses. Limiting our rhythmic vocabulary to eighth notes helps us to not resort to rhythmic tricks to create energy or momentum in a melodic line, and helps us to focus more simply on what we hear the next note to be. If we are hearing and playing a strong logical and organically evolving eighth note melody, it will have plenty of forward moving energy. We won't need to resort to tricks of any kind, rhythmic ones or unmotivated technical displays to drive the music forward. Such displays when not genuinely motivated by the music, not coming from inside the music, amount to nothing more than what they are, a display of technique.........better left in the practice room. Let us remember that the eighth note line is at the heart of our jazz vocabulary, its meat and potatoes. Let us allow the music to evolve and emerge from that place, that foundation, and let our technique serve the music and its expression.

What To Say.........

All communications are made up of phrases, and to communicate musically or verbally, we have to know what we want to say. It truly is that simple.

The hard part is figuring out what we want to express. To try and do that without complete confidence in our knowledge of the subject matter at hand, in our case a musical composition, and our relationship to it, is nothing more than folly. We are truly cheating ourselves if we approach learning in anything less than a comprehensive way, regardless of our level of experience and knowledge. Doing our due diligence is the only way to find out how good we can be, and it's the only way we can express ourselves in meaningful, coherent musical phrases.

> *"I have discovered that jazz is not nearly as much about playing what you know, but musically going to those places you have never been before. When I first started out it was very scary to think this way - but with experience, I have become very comfortable with the freedom that comes from simply playing from phrase to phrase".*

> **—FRED HERSCH**

Hearing In Phrases

Perspective: point of view, viewpoint, frame of reference, approach, way of looking at, interpretation, angle, slant, attitude, position, vista, panorama, outlook. If you look up perspective in the dictionary these are some of the synonyms or synonymous phrases that you'll see. What does perspective have to do with phrasing? Perhaps everything.

When you begin your solo, (or you begin playing a Chopin Nocturne), where are you? What are you seeing, hearing, feeling? Where are you going? Do you have a destination in mind, in ear? What will you say? A word or two, an utterance of some kind? A grunt, a yell, a scream, a question, an answer? The telling of a joke or the beginning of a story?

What's your perspective, your point of view? Are you at the beginning or the end? Are you in the middle? Has something already been said? Are you responding to or initiating the conversation? How long will you play? A short piece? Many pages? How many bars are you playing? Are you saying something for the first bar only? The first chord only? What is your intention? Are you playing a bar at a time, maybe two?

Finally the sixty-four thousand dollar question; are you playing a phrase? Hoping to?

If playing a phrase is what we want to do, if playing and hearing in phrases is what we want to do, then that must be our perspective. So when we make our first utterance, our perspective is not that of the first bar or chord only, but at a minimum, it is that of an entire phrase, whether four bars or eight bars or whatever our understanding of the music tells us. We spoke earlier of space as it relates to phrasing. Having the perspective of a phrase, and then that of the entire form as our point of view, helps us to feel good with space, with silences, with waiting and being patient with the music. There's no need to say it all in the first bar, on the first chord, no need to rush things, as we've got a whole phrase to work with, indeed the whole form to work with. With this way of looking at and hearing music, we hear our ideas in relationship to a bigger context, a whole. The first notes we play aren't isolated thoughts but part of a bigger picture, a grander scheme, a longer conversation, a story we are telling that takes a chorus or two or three to tell, takes the whole nocturne to tell. If we're improvising on a standard tune, now maybe a difference between the first A and the second A starts to emerge. Maybe the bridge feels different than it did before and maybe just maybe the last A feels like the last A and not just like the first or second, and maybe the feeling of an entire chorus has taken shape.

Perspective......................................

Time

Music is an up gesture, not an earthbound one........... it needs to dance.

I like to think of the beat as being round, a circle if you will. If we accept that premise, and draw a line through the center of the circle, we can see that within that beat there is room in front of and behind that center line, i.e. the middle of the beat. So there is room for us to play on either the front or backside of the beat, and not be rushing or dragging. As always it's a question of degree. If we play too far forward we *will* rush, and too far back we *will* be a weight on the time.

While we all have our natural tendencies as to how we feel time, be it on top, laid back or down the middle, it's important that we know how these different places within the beat feel. I think it's fair to say that all three of the above described time feels have their place in musical interpretation and expression, it's a matter of deciding what's appropriate for the style, and what fits what we want to "say". The best case scenario is that we very intentionally practice playing in all three places described, know how they feel to us, and are then able to use them expressively as needed.

Group Time

Since we spend most of our time playing in ensembles of one sort or another, I think a word about "group time sense" is worthwhile. So what do I mean by "group time sense?" I mean that everyone in the group is responsible for the time, a shared responsibility, and everyone in the group needs to be willing to make the very subtle adjustments necessary to arrive at a solid feel that everyone can hang on to. I had a discussion about time one day with my friend, the late Carl Saunders, absolutely one of the best trumpet players and musicians in the world. He talked about this as "tuning the time", the goal being for the group to become one with it. I'll say this again I'm sure in a different context, it's not about being right or correct, and clinging to what we individually feel is the right tempo. Barring obviously bad playing as regards the time that is too severe to compensate for, there are subtle and reasonable adjustments that I think all great groups make. A lot of the time I don't think it's even overtly conscious, but happens intuitively, a result of how closely players are listening to each other, and how strong their desire is to play together, to feel it together, as one. When this is happening the music feels great, both to play and to listen too. From the playing standpoint it feels relaxed, unhurried, like it "plays itself" regardless of tempo, and it feels like you can employ the three different time placements talked about above, without destroying the overall feel. Under these circumstances, the group time sense is locked and solid, so when you're taking a solo you can play with the time a bit without fear of actually moving it one way or the other. You can lean against it, push it a bit, and then return to the center of the beat or to where the group is. If the group feel hasn't been established, it's very difficult to do any of this without adversely affecting the time.

Truly the most important thing is that the band plays time together. If the band in question feels it on top, that's fine, they'll be able to maintain that feeling without rushing. I think Chick Corea's time feel is wonderful, and it feels on top to me, sounds and feels great, and his bands manifest this magnificently. The heralded Basie band is noted for it's swinging laid back feel, and that band always felt just wonderful. Listen to Stan Getz's solo on a live recording of Stella By Starlight. The cd is called "Anniversary". Listen to where he places his eighth notes, quarter note triplets etc., and listen to where his sixteenth note double time lines sit. This solo is a great example of what we're talking about. As Stan expresses himself in the time, the band is rock solid and the group time sense is always in tact.

A Little More About Time

Every beat is not the same. Think of conducting patterns and how conductors physically manifest and communicate a tempo and feeling for time and meter to an orchestra. Every beat is in a different place and the last beat regardless of time signature is always an up gesture.

As I spoke earlier about the importance of hearing pitch relationships, harmonic relationships, their forward movement from one to the other, we must hear and feel time in the same way. I say again, that music doesn't jump up and down in place, it moves forward, horizontally. That applies to all musical concepts or components, time, rhythm and meter included. So beat one is different from beat two and two different from three and so on. This is a musical application of Arsis and Thesis. If beat one is a point of arrival, the "thesis" in our system of musical meter, then the remaining beats in a bar of music are moving forward, creating an upward arc or gesture, or "arsis" to lead us across the bar line and into the beginning of the next bar.

If we expand this interpretation of arsis and thesis to a four bar phrase, we now have a larger arc, another layer of movement. Then each bar in the phrase holds a unique place in a forward rolling circle of time.

Being in touch with this larger time sense is critically important. We can develop a very visceral sense of time, of phrase, so we physically feel when four bars, eight bars have been completed. Remember, no phrasing - no form, no feeling of phrase - no feeling of form.

Music is an up gesture, not an earthbound one, it needs to dance.

Harmonic Skeletons

What are the harmonies in a tune that are essential? Conversely, what chords could we do without? What harmonies are destinations and which are ones that we "pass through" along the way? If we can answer these questions well, I think we will have a pretty good understanding of what the harmonic skeleton is. Having that understanding puts us in touch with phrase structure and form, which broadens our perspective and helps us to hear the harmonic relationships in question. Most importantly, this awareness helps us to *hear in phrases,* instead of being focused on one chord at a time.

Let's look at a tune by the great jazz pianist and composer Kenny Baron.

"Voyage"

The tune is in F minor so we're starting on the one chord in that key and our first destination is.................the Bb minor chord in bar five, or the four chord in F minor. So the first part of our trip is simply going from one minor to four minor harmonically. How do we get there? We have one bar of F#m and one bar of F7 to negotiate before arriving at our four chord. Upon first glance it seems we have two stops along the way to Bb minor, well, hopefully not stops but streets we have to navigate. Is there a way to simplify our conception of the first four bars? In order to do that I have to see if I can find some sort of relationship between F#m and F7. Again at first glance it may seem that there isn't one as I have two harmonies a half step apart. But upon further inspection, I see that there are some common tones between the two harmonies. A is the third in both chords, F while being the root of F7 could also be the maj7 of F#m, the Eb or seventh of the F7 chord could also be the sixth of F#m. So there are three common tones, A, F, and Eb. Is there a scale relationship? Yes there is. An altered scale is the same as an ascending melodic minor scale, the only difference being the note from which we start. For F# melodic minor we start from the root of the chord or F#. For an altered dominant chord, we would find the related melodic minor shape, or its altered scale, by looking at the melodic minor scale that starts a half step above the root of the dominant seventh chord in question, in this case an F7 chord. So an F7 altered scale and an F# melodic minor scale are one in the same. Understanding that relationship simplifies our aural conception, and makes it easier to hear horizontally towards our intended musical destination. Now we can look at our journey from Fm to Bbm in bar five more simply. Now it becomes 2 bars of I, Fm, 2 bars of V7/iv (F#m and F7) and arriving at iv, Bbm in bar five.

So we've combined two harmonies into what I refer to as a "dominant area". Now instead of hearing two harmonies as being separate, I hear them as being related, and functionally united in purpose, getting us to the iv chord.

Moving forward in the music, after the Bbm harmony we are headed back to a cadence on i, Fm. We get there by way of a iim7b5 - V7b9 of Fm. The Bbm harmony in bar five is a pivot chord, both a point of arrival and a point of departure back to Fm. The relationship between Bbm and Gm7b5 should be quite obvious, basically the same harmony given a different color by the changing of the root. Now, why not think of a iim7 - V7 as a dominant area? No reason not to, so again this broadens our conception. Now it's once again not two separate harmonies to consider, but two related harmonies with a common purpose, to function in a dominant relationship to F minor. As a result the A sections of the composition are conceptually reduced to i - V7/iv - iv - V7/i - i. All in all a pretty simple harmonic proposition. Let's go on to the bridge.

The B section of the composition starts on Dbmaj7, the VI chord in Fm. Typically that harmony might lead us back to V7 and then back to i. But instead it launches us on an ascending chromatic succession of Major keys, from Db Major to E Major. Each new key arrival is preceded by a iim7 - V7, again not two separate chords but a "dominant area" in that key. So after the Dbmaj7, we have two bars of D Major, two bars of Eb Major, two bars of E Major, and then one bar of V7 of i which takes us to our last A section of the tune. Before we discuss the common-alities between Emaj7 and C7, let's review our thinking as regards the bridge. We are basically reducing it to a chromatic series of Major key centers, climbing from Db to E Major. There are diatonic iim7 -V7s there as well. Perhaps we can say that considering the ii-V harmony is 'level 2" of our conception, and "level one", the most basic skeleton, has us breaking things down simply into key centers. Level two now brings into consideration the related dominant areas, and how we might treat them.

We could treat them diatonically, without any dominant scale alterations and just stay in Major scale territory, al-lowing the ii - V to then color that Major tonality and get us to the I Major harmony. We could also just treat the ii -V as the dominant area that it is, and ignore the iim7, and treat those bars as V7 chords. In that case, we now possibly have an entire bar of some kind of V7 related scales or harmonies to work with. We can also acknowledge the iim7s, and treat those bars as such, incorporating the iim7 chords into our harmonic and linear conception. These are just a few of the many dominant color possibilities we might consider. Before we summarize, let's go back and take a look at the relationship between Emaj7 and C7.

When I'm looking for relationships in music, I try and look at and for everything I can find, no matter how small, obvious or seemingly insignificant. Let me say categorically, there are no musical relationships or connections that you can make between one thing and another, that are ever insignificant. When I look for relationships in music, I always find much more than I think I will, it never fails, and you will too, I guarantee it.

So, back to the music, an E is the leading tone to F, and an E is the third of a C7 chord. The third of the Emaj7 chord is a G#, which if put into a C7 chord makes it a C7 augmented chord, and that G# is also an Ab and also the third degree of our tonic key, F minor. The other note of consequence in a C7 chord is the 7th, the Bb. That Bb could also be looked at as an A#, the raised fourth of an E Lydian scale, also the fourth degree of an F minor scale. Is there a scale relationship to be found? By now you know the answer is going to be yes. If we look at a C7 Altered scale and an E Lydian scale, we find that *all notes are in common* accept for one, the B natural in the E Lydian scale does not occur in a C7 Altered scale. Other than that, all scale tones are common to both scales: E, F#, G#, Bb, C# and D#, six out of seven scale tones in common. If we don't go the Lydian route on the Emaj7 chord and go Major, we still have five common scale tones, a significant number by any measure. (This is the same harmonic avenue used from the bridge back to the A section in the standard "All The Things You Are".) So now again we can get two seemingly unrelated harmonies into a common functional area, a dominant one leading us back to home base, in this case F minor.

Conceiving of and hearing this composition now becomes easier. What initially looked like a complicated and difficult tune to negotiate, now feels a bit more accessible. Now it's a i to iv to i for the A sections, and a bridge that passes chromatically through some Major key centers. I don't mean to suggest in any way that Voyage is an easy tune, or that to pull off a successful solo on any composition is easy. What I am saying is that our conceptual understanding of a composition, of music, is at the heart of a process that hopefully leads us to meaningful musical expression. I am saying that the broader our conception, the more possibilities we will see and hear. Also, and most importantly, it helps us to have musical perspective, i.e. to understand the following questions: "What harmonies are essential and which are more like colors along the way"? "What are my points of arrival and what are my points of departure"?

 The answers to these questions and more, lie in our conceptual understanding of the music we are trying to learn and play and perform.

Improvisation

Improvising is a practiced skill. In my teaching experience, I have found that many students seem to think it's just supposed to happen for them. Beyond some understanding of chord - scale relationships they do not venture very far, if at all, into deeper levels of musical understanding and analysis. I've already spoken to the importance of intimately knowing in every way the music we wish to play, so I won't be redundant as to all the reasons why this is so vitally important.........but I will add that our improvising must be tune specific, composition specific, not chord change specific.........hence the critical importance, of knowing the unique characteristics of the composition at hand. *We don't improvise on chord changes, we improvise on the totality of a musical composition.*

Practicing Improvisation

How do we practice something that is supposed to be a spontaneous musical expression? How do we work at it and not have our performances turn into perfunctory regurgitations of what we've practiced? That's a good question, and I never said this would be easy.

I think to a certain extent it's a mind set that keeps the above mentioned quandary from happening. When it's time to perform, we need to have a clean ear and an open mind, free of preconceived or practiced ideas. We need to be in a place to hear in the moment, and respond to what we play in a way that is specific to the moment at hand. We also need to trust.........trust that we will hear............trust that what we've been practicing will be there, but as part of an intuitive musical flow, instead of as a set of predetermined ideas. I realize that what I'm proposing may seem or feel risky, and I suppose in a way it is............but how else will we learn to trust ourselves? If I'm recalling something specific that I practiced and want to play it in an improvised solo, then I'm playing from memory, and that's different from hearing and playing in the moment.............the two are mutually exclusive, so we have to choose...............we can either throw caution to the wind and trust ourselves to hear what we hear and let the notes fall where they may, or we can try and play from memory...........but we can't do both, we can't switch back and forth from one mind set to another, one way of hearing and then another and expect to make music that flows in an organic way, where ideas are developed and related to each other, where phrasing and form resultantly emerge.

So how can we practice to foster this kind of open approach to improvising? I believe we have to practice in ways that inform our hearing, and our conception of how music works. If we work within that context, then we are not practicing things to remember, melodies to regurgitate, but rather we are practicing music conceptually, practicing how we hear music emerge and develop.

For example, one way to practice phrasing is to follow the phrase structure of the melody of a tune. Is it written in four bar phrases? Questions and answers? I can practice those things. I can practice playing in four bar phrases and question and answer phrasing within that structure. *What I am after is the feeling of a phrase.* I want to hear in phrases, and be absolutely specific as to what note is the beginning of my phrase and what note is the end of my phrase. I want to internalize the phrase structure of the music I'm working on, so I practice the concept of phrasing. I want to take into performance an ability to hear in phrases, to hear conversationally, i.e. questions and answers, and to develop a visceral feeling for four bars, eight bars, sixteen bars, thirty two bars, and end up with an internalized melodic structure and sense of form, from which I can create my variations. I want my abstractions to be deeply rooted in and connected to the composition. That is a very important idea.

As another example of practicing a concept, a common practice in bebop melodic lines is the outlining of chord tones in a variety of ways. So I can practice outlining chord tones, approaching them and "surrounding" them from above and below, chromatically and/or diatonically so I can learn to hear what that sounds and feels like. As I internalize these shapes and sounds, I can then begin to incorporate them into the way that I hear and play. *I'm learning to internalize a concept.* That is different than learning some specific bebop lines to regurgitate. Even if we were to commit to memory some such lines, I believe if we are coming from a conceptual place of learning, should one of these memorized lines "pop up" in an improvisation, there is a much better chance that it, or some part of it, will emerge more organically. There's a better chance it will sound more like it's "ours", rather than it feeling like it's something we've learned and are now regurgitating. When the latter is the case, the idea often feels unmotivated and usually sounds out of context.

We each have to learn to hear our own way. So we practice to inform our conception of music and improvisation. We practice to learn to express ourselves, with the same twelve notes we all use, in our own way. It is nothing but folly to think it is even possible, or artistically worthwhile, to learn to hear and feel music like anyone else but ourselves. We have to use what we learn, what we internalize, to inform our own unique voices. I want to sound like me, and I want you to sound like you.

Importantly, we use what we practice to inform our improvisations. Whatever we digest in the way of vocabulary, harmonic possibilities, transcription study, we must internalize and integrate it all into the way we each hear. We will all digest this information differently and each use it differently, each hear it differently, according to our individual aesthetics and sense of expression. We will and in fact must, develop our own relationships to the musical sounds that we make, the harmonies and rhythms and melodic shapes that uniquely speak to us. The sounds we make have to mean something to us.............why else would we make them?

Melodic Variation

It is essential for us to know the melody of a composition in order to have any hope of successfully improvising on it. The vast majority of what we do as improvisors is theme and variation, and so it is obvious that step one should be knowing the theme. If we are going to abstract, we need to intimately know that from which we are abstracting.

There is a very direct link between our understanding of the "theme" and our ability to abstract from it, to render variations of it. The greater our understanding of the fundamental, the greater our ability to abstract. I believe this to be a directly proportional relationship. Picasso could render an abstraction of a bull or a human face because he knew how to draw each realistically very very well. Step one is learning the music, the melody and harmony as it is written, in a very intimate way.

When we set about to "vary" a melody, let's take into consideration not just pitch variation but rhythmic variation as well. A rhythmic variation of a melodic phrase is a valid variation, so our variation can be solely rhythmic, it can be primarily a pitch variation, or some combination of the two. One of the ways I like to practice melodic variation is to simply follow the shape of the melody, its skeleton of you will. Yes, melodies have skeletons too. The simplest way of looking at a melody's shape is to look at the starting note of the phrase, the highest or lowest note of the phrase depending on the direction of it, and the ending note of the phrase. Now my task is to fashion melodic ideas that follow that same contour. This approach also keeps me in touch again, with the phrase structure of the composition, and reinforces my hearing and playing of phrases that make sense. I also think it reinforces the melody in us, in a different way than a literal playing of it does. For me I always feel like the melody is playing in my head, on a separate track if you will, allowing me to always stay in touch with it, no matter how far from it I may seem to stray. It remains a point of reference as I create variations and abstractions of it. In his autobiography Miles Davis tells a story of Thelonious Monk not liking the way he Miles, played on "'Round Midnight". Monk told him he couldn't hear the melody when Miles improvised. I take that to mean that Monk wasn't hearing enough of a relationship between the two, between what Miles was improvising and the written melody. Even when an accomplished improvisor is getting very abstract, they seem to always have a way of keeping us in touch with how they hear a relationship between what they are playing and the melody. It may be as obvious as a direct quote of the melody, or something close to it, or a rhythmic reference or an important melody note that starts a new section of the form perhaps. All of that helps keep the relationship between theme and variation alive.

Don't Avoid The Obvious

Often in my experience with students, they seem to have the idea that when it's time to take a solo on a tune, they need to do something completely unrelated to the composition at hand. Sometimes it seems as if they feel it's cheating to use the melody of a tune when improvising on it. They seem to think they must start from scratch so to speak, as if prior to their solo, no music had been played. Instead of conceiving of their solo as a continuation of the music that's already been played, they seem to think and feel that they are starting over. Well nothing could be farther from the truth. At a minimum a theme has been stated, i.e. the melody has been played, and possibly a solo also has been played by another member of the ensemble. So perhaps we have both a theme and a variation to work with, to respond to. The soloist that precedes us if that is indeed the case, hopefully influences us as well. That's potentially a lot of material to work with, a lot of music to respond to.

So let's be clear, our task is not to run from the material at hand but to get deeper into it, to unearth its subtext. Our way in is through what the composition gives us to work with, its melody and harmony and rhythms and meter and lyrics if they apply. The textures and dynamics, our feelings for and about the music and how we relate to the sounds it has to offer, these are all aspects of the music that inform our conception of it. So our job is not to run away from the music but rather to run towards it and into it with all the understanding, knowledge and awareness we can muster. One might say that all that I've just stated above is obvious, that what we need is all there before us in the music we are trying to play, so there's no need to so consciously concern ourselves with it. If something is that obvious and so right there in front of us, then it must just take care of itself, automatically happen. Well, I think the obvious doesn't just take care of itself, quite to the contrary, *we have to take care of it,* give it life, use it, make it ours.

Cadences are another obvious thing in music, and they don't take care of themselves either. Too many times I hear them go unattended, left to fend for themselves, as if they can........left with unresolved melodies or ending notes that bear no relationship to the notes from whence they came............or the interjection of what is deemed to be a "hip" note instead of what would be the obvious choice. Let's understand something, there is no hierarchy of hipness with notes. The tonic can be as hip as any extension you can come up with, none of the twelve are any "hipper" than any of the others. I don't even like the word "hip" and what it implies as regards music, and jazz improvisation in particular. What we need to be concerned with is an organic progression of a phrase and its' completion, and achieving a cadence, a sense of tension and release. The note that happens to do that in the moment, is simply the one. It's the one for that moment and it doesn't matter if it's the tonic or the third or fifth or ninth or the sixth or the sharped eleventh, it simply doesn't matter. What matters is that it finishes the phrase, achieves the cadence, and says what we want to say. So end the phrase, make the cadence, and don't avoid the obvious choice because you've decided that a particular chord tone that you hear the phrase heading towards isn't "hip" enough. *Don't judge it, just play it, play what you hear, find the logic, respond to where the music wants to go.*

Listening

Hearing something and listening to it are two different things. Learning how to listen is as important as anything we do as musicians.

Listening to ourselves.........to the entire sound of the band........to how what we are playing fits into the whole sound.............to the time............how is the time being felt.........are the bass and drums feeling the time the same way.....is one of them ahead of the other.........are they locked.......where is my time feel in relation to theirs.........how is the balance...........am I hearing too much of myself or not enough............... the bass.......the drums.......can I hear the singer...........what do I need to hear more of........less of.................

What's my response to the music I'm hearing......playing........how does it make me feel.............what is it saying to me and what am I saying to it............with it............energetic in your face music............intro-spective ballad.........harmony that moves you......... a melody you wish you wrote............

words that cut like a knife.........make you cry............ make you smile.............words you can relate to.......... your story............lyrics that feel true............lots of levels............layers of music and sound................ am I inside all of this............flowing with it............ letting it emerge...............

knowing what to say.........what I want to say.........am I hearing the conversation.........the questions............ the answers............

Practicing

What do we practice? Technique? Sight Reading? Reper-toire? Improvisation? Transposing? Voicing and voice leading? Playing with a metronome? Memorization?

All of the above and whatever is on our plate profession-ally or academically that needs specific attention is what we practice. It is important to have a list, to have priori-ties, and to stay in touch with everything that needs our attention on a consistent basis. Priorities will shift, but as they do, everything we need to practice has to stay actively on our radar. As an example, let's say we haven't sight read anything in a couple of weeks, hopefully a light bulb of awareness turns on and we then spend some time sight reading. The same applies to all the skills we must hone and maintain.

I would like to take a moment to stress the importance of practicing and maintaining fundamental musicianship skills. To draw an athletic comparison, when professional baseball players show up for spring training, they practice taking ground balls and fly balls, hitting and bunting practice, who to throw the ball to in different situations. These are all fundamental baseball skills that they've all been practicing and executing since they were children. They don't show up and say "I already know how to do these things so I don't need to practice them". We practice fundamentals so we can depend on them in performance, it's as simple as that.

Piano Technique

For me the most important goal of technical practice is hand balance and finger support, relaxation, proper use of the wrist, and understanding the whole playing mechanism. The goal should not be to develop speed. Speed is a by product that will emerge somewhat effortlessly if we are using our playing mechanism properly. If the proper foundation is not in place, then practicing scales and arpeggios and whatever exercises one may do too fast, is only going to reinforce bad habits and possibly cause injury by over stressing some part of our hand, wrist or arm. We need to practice slowly enough so we can pay attention to how our hands, wrists and arms are working and feeling.

There are different schools of thought on piano technique, but I think there are some common fundamentals we can agree on. First, however we think our playing mechanism should be used, I think we all would agree that it must be used in a coordinated and relaxed fashion. Secondly, we want to play on the pads of our fingers and not on the tips of the fingers, we don't want to be too perpendicular to the keys. Third, our wrists have to be free and supple, so they can move from side to side and up and down as needed, so as to balance or position the hand so it can support all fingers as needed, the fourth and fifth fingers in particular. Also we need our wrists and hands to help us shape larger physical gestures so we can respond to the changing topography of the piano, and to shape phrases. Music is not a one note at a time proposition, so we don't want to succumb to a one note - one finger at a time kind of playing, from either a technical or a musical standpoint. Fourth, getting to the bottom of the key bed is also a fundamental concept we can all agree on, as it is essential to producing a centered, focused tone at the piano.

So as you can see there's a lot to pay attention to and be aware of when we're playing the piano. Practicing technique too fast just doesn't allow us enough time to be in touch with how our wrists and hands and arms are working and feeling. So don't worry about speed, if you get the relaxed coordination part right, the speed and facility you need will be there. Also, let's remember that playing fast is not just a physical activity, it's an aural one, we need to learn to "hear fast" as well. The fingers respond to what we hear, not the other way around, so the hearing part needs to be practiced as well. Technique must be aurally driven. Another way of saying this perhaps is to say that technique doesn't determine the sounds we want to make, *the sounds we want to make drive the development of our individual technique.*

More Thoughts on Piano Technique

We don't play with our fingers..........that's just where the music comes out.

Our physical approach needs to be compatible, or in sync, with the musical gestures at hand. To that end, we first must understand that music can't be dealt with on a one note at a time basis, but rather we must understand music in larger pieces, phrases and gestures if you will. If we are going to match a physical gesture with a musical one, we first must understand the musical gestures of the music we wish to play, the arc of phrases. Once we have such understanding, we can then proceed to come up with a physical approach that will best express the music.

All we need do is look at a conductors patterns to see that music is not intended to proceed as a flat line, but rather as a set of nuanced ups and downs and indeed circular gestures. For the pianist these shapes need to be reflected and shaped physically, with the wrist and the hand, with the support of the arms, matching the circular, up and down gestures or phrases of the music. Again, our wrist and hand movements need to match the musical gesture of the phrase. So we're looking to match the shape of musical gestures with the shape of our physical gestures. As I've said, the wrist is central to this movement, and must be free to move up and down to the degree necessary, and side to side as well to balance the hand so it can support the fingers that are working.

It's not possible to do any of this if we are too tense. In my own personal experience as a student and subsequently as a teacher, a frozen wrist is more often than not the culprit. I think this happens because we try to play with our fingers only. That approach freezes the wrist and cuts off any flow of energy from the shoulders on down, creating an "energy dam" at the wrist.

What if we change our perception? Instead of thinking that we play the piano with our fingers, what if we say that the fingers just happen to be where the music comes out, that *they are the end point of a process rather than the initiators of one?*

I don't mean to suggest that the fingers are free from technical responsibility, they are not. It's best to play on the pads of the fingers, that means the fifth finger too, not on it's side. We also need to not break our nail joints. We also have to balance the hand properly behind the fingers .... and that takes us right back to the wrist being free to move side to side, to properly balance the hand behind and in support of the fingers that are in use at any given moment.

So let me be clear, we don't and in fact cannot shape musical gestures with our fingers. We need the larger muscles for that, with the help and guidance of a supple wrist. We need a free flow of energy to play music.

Tension and Release

Doing anything physical at all is a continuous cycle of tension and relaxation. When we walk our weight transfers from foot to foot or leg to leg, and as one hits the ground the other relaxes and comes up and so on. If we didn't relax a leg during this process, we'd all walk around like Frankensteins.

Playing the piano is no different. We cannot collect tension as we play. We must release it as we play, a continuous cycle of use it and relax it, tension and release. Importantly, it only takes a millisecond to release the tension we've used to play something, so the release happens rather immediately after use. If we do this, our hands should feel the same at the end of a performance as they did at the beginning. If they don't, you are not releasing tension as you play but rather, collecting it. As a result, you are probably playing in a constant state of some level of unnecessary tension.

Sight Reading

Shapes and patterns......shapes and patterns......what is the **form** of this music......**texture**......chordal...... contrapuntal...........two voices...........scaler......... arpeggiated......what are the **rhythms**......most prominent subdivisions.........**meter**...........does it appear to have a lot of syncopations......**melodic shape**...... by step.........skips......leaps......fourths......fifths...... octaves......**style**......impressionist......jazz......classical......baroque......romantic......**dynamics**........... will my hands be staying in one register or moving over a wide range of the piano...............

These are all things I want to know about before I concern myself with the name of a note. It seems if we get primarily concerned with pitch recognition, most all of the above goes out the window. So most importantly, when you practice sight reading, do not stop to correct pitch. Keep your eyes and ears moving forward, and yes your ears too. It is important to keep your aural imagination active. Allow yourself to imagine what the music sounds like before you start playing it. Secondly, look for patterns of any kind or length. You see we must learn to digest music in patterns and shapes, more than one note at a time. Use your ability to improvise to help you to keep going in time. I believe the only way we get a sense of how a piece of music sounds is to keep moving through it in time, regardless of how many "right" notes we play. I think it also important to put in front of yourself music that is easy for you to read, moderately difficult, and music that is very difficult for you to read. Reading music that is easy for you, or perhaps a piece you've learned before, I believe helps to reinforce our pattern recognition. With music that is very complex for us, I think it forces us to deal with shapes and patterns and textures more exclusively, and forces us to use our ability to improvise to get an idea of what the music is about, i.e. what it feels like to play it, and what it sounds like. I think we can get those ideas regardless of how pitch accurate we are, if we keep moving and respond to the shapes, textures, rhythms and dynamics that we see. This approach I think is particularly important when reading a piece for the first time that we intend to learn and bring to performance level.

What we want upon a first reading is to get an idea of what the music is like, to get an idea of the whole, a gestalt if you will. Once we've established for ourselves a sense of the whole, we can then work on details and refine those details and inform our gestalt as we go. I'd like to have a sense of the whole first, it gives me a place to put things. The other way is to work on parts or sections one at a time, and then try to understand how they fit together, to assemble them. For me that's backwards learning, a backward process. If we were going to build a new house, we'd need a blueprint, an architectural design to work from. While some changes to the design may occur as construction proceeds, we certainly wouldn't start putting up walls and building rooms without first at least having an idea of how these rooms fit together, or how many we need.

Repertoire

There are levels of knowing a piece of music. There's music that is completely new to us, music we know enough to play, and music we have lived with for some time, know by memory and can sit down and play without any concern as to whether or not we know it.

All three levels of "knowing" present different kinds of learning opportunities. There is learning that is unique or particular to each level. What we can learn from and with music that we have lived with for some time and feel like we know intimately is simply not accessible in the earlier stages of knowing. They each have their purpose in the process, each offering a certain level of understanding, requiring certain skills. I feel very strongly that we must have the third level, music we feel like we know, that we can explore and play in a variety of ways, music that we love to play. Having such music in us provides a perspective on the process. If we don't venture deeply into knowing, we may not be aware that all we've been doing is scratching the surface. If that's the case, then we don't get to the deeper questions of conception and interpretation, of exploring our own voices and artistry.

Voicing

Voicing is contextual........where are these voices coming from and going to.........what is the melody doing...........does the melody contain chord tones............extensions........how might the rhythm of the melody and the harmonic rhythm itself impact our voicing choices...........what is the texture of the music........... ....does it need to stay consistent or change.........how does register affect what the music needs.....................

The great jazz pianist Jimmy Rowles told me in a brief talk about voicing chords, in his unique and somewhat rough and raspy tone, "they're voices, the chord tones are all voices". What great musical perspective, among the best ever imparted to me. When we think in those terms, it immediately shifts our perspective from vertical to horizontal. We are less likely to think of voices, chord tones, as being static, but rather they start to come alive, need to move forward, need to sing. We begin to hear their potential for movement, and must always consider and take care of that potential.

This question of chord extensions, added tensions, is one that always comes up with students when we discuss or work on voicing chords. If we consider the above mentioned contextual considerations, and view them and hear them as additional voices and not static chord tones, then the question kind of answers itself. If they serve a musical purpose beyond that of just making a beautiful vertical sound, and serve the forward movement of the music, then choosing to add to a harmony, or add a voice, becomes a reasonable choice.

Our decision must be purposeful and must hold up to musical scrutiny.........does the choice, to add a note or notes serve the music? Does the addition heighten the tension and release of the phrase, or create more forward movement than would otherwise be there? Is there an expression that is satisfied by the choice, something more we wanted to say, perhaps in a different way............these are questions that need be asked and answered.

Another issue that comes up with students that I think is very relevant to our above discussion, is the idea of using incomplete voicing, or a voicing that doesn't contain all of the chord tones. Often students try and force all the chord tones into a voicing and the results are often less than musical. We end up with unnecessary doublings, and sounds that are often too muddy, with close intervals that are simply too low in register. Again, this pertains to horizontal hearing and conception, and also to texture.

Shell voicings are an example of an incomplete or partial voicing. Typically, playing the third and the seventh of a chord is perhaps the most common form of a shell voicing, but this is not the only "shell" voicing that's possible. There are others that need to include the third or seventh but not both, that will still provide a voice leading sensibility. Sometimes a consistent shape will provide enough horizontal logic as well, even though the usual movement of thirds and sevenths is absent from the texture. We could use two or three note shapes as well, be it in a close voicing, or spread out, and so on. Another concept or idea I'd like to suggest is that we need to "see the harmony all over the place" so to speak, and not just see or know chords in only a prescribed set of positions and inversions. That can be an okay place to start to learn voicing, but we must not stop there. We have to keep up the search for different sounds and shapes, different textural possibilities. So the goal is ultimately about developing flexibility, so we see, hear and know a variety of ways to create harmonic color that moves forward with a sense of tension and release.

The Physical Part

From a purely physical standpoint, as piano players, our hands do need to learn shapes, the shapes of chords in differing topographies. Repetition is the only way for fundamental chord shapes to become second nature to us. This repetition must be consistent, and that means everyday until we can start to access them quickly, on the spur of a musical moment. That being said, repetition alone is only part of the way we need to practice voicing. It is worth reiterating that it is imperative that we explore harmonic colors and textures that require different shapes, different combinations of chord tones and extensions, that produce different kinds of sounds. Finally, it is critically important that we do this work *in a musical context,* in musical ways, in the context of musical compositions, always remembering that collectively and individually, chord tones are voices that want and need to move forward, horizontally.

Comping

The term "comping" comes from the word accompanying, so it simply means to accompany. How to best do that in a jazz setting is often hard for inexperienced players to figure out, and sometimes for experienced players as well.

If we were recording, and we listened back to just the accompanying tracks of piano, bass and drums let's say, without hearing the soloist or the melody, we should still hear something musical that stands on its own, even though we're missing the main melodic voice. We should still hear phrasing, and we should still hear a melodic sensibility. If we are playing a succession of chords, the top notes of our voicings is our melody, or counter-melody. So when we are in an accompanying role, our musical responsibilities remain the same as they are when we are the lead instrument or voice, we just manifest them differently.

It is not the job of the person comping to relentlessly lay out the harmony. You don't have to play every chord.

Everyone should hear the harmony whether it's played or not. Another potential pitfall is to get stuck in the same register, which usually begets the same texture over and over and over again. Don't get stuck in the middle!!! There's high and low and all the in betweens and lots of varieties of texture that are possible, so don't be afraid to explore them.

I think comping is best when it is in conversation with the soloist. The soloist is leading the conversation for sure, and we are listening intently to what is being said and supporting that point of view with our responses. Our responses can be primarily rhythmic or melodic, and always a combination of both to some degree. Sometimes the best response is patient silence, allowing space and time for the soloist to express themselves.

Sometimes the best response is none at all. At other times being more interactive is the most supportive thing we can do. We may find ourselves in direct rhythmic and/or melodic conversation with the soloist. It all depends on how we listen and digest what we're hearing, and how we interpret what the soloist is saying. Also, and importantly, if there are other instruments involved, say drums and bass, we all have to listen just as intently to each other as we do the soloist. All accompanists involved have a shared responsibility to listen and to hear and to play phrases. Everyone has to be intimately engaged in the process, in the music, listening deeply to each other and the soloist. It is not the time to just mindlessly play time or play chords or walk a bass line and wait for it to be your turn to solo. All of that is exactly what comping is not. *Whatever our role, our level of concentration and focus should never waiver. From the first sound until the last, whether we are playing the melody, soloing, accompanying or counting bars of rest, our level of engagement and interest should be the same.* It's all part of the music, all part of the vibe, all interrelated...............all critically important.

Memorization

Playing from memory is like taking a mirror to our learning process. It is where we find out just how thorough that process has been. It represents the culmination of our learning.

I have a proposition for you. What if instead of saying "I'm going to learn to play this piece or tune", we said "I'm going to internalize this music"? For me the word internalize is more visceral, the word learning more intellectual. (Visceral as defined in the dictionary relates to *deep inward feelings rather than to intellect.*)

I don't think anyone would argue the fact that the goal is to internalize the music we want to learn, play and perform. We learn about the music to facilitate internalizing it. So just learning it is not the end game, *the end game is internalization.* So why not start the process that way, with that being the goal from the beginning? I believe if we begin our learning from that perspective, it will significantly impact our learning process, making it a more comprehensive one from the start.

Internalization implicitly implies more than just muscle memory. I think we know from our own personal experiences that muscle memory alone will not get us to a secure memorization and resultant performance. I know I have had performance experiences where I unfortunately discovered mid-performance that my primary way of knowing the music at hand was that I learned where my fingers should go. Unfortunately, when one of them inadvertently went somewhere else, I was lost and it was almost impossible to recover without seriously compromising the performance.

So simply put, we need to know more about the music we plan to perform. We need to understand and importantly hear, all the musical relationships that make it what it is, that make it whole. Ideally, we want to be able to discuss, explain, or write a paper about any and all aspects of a composition that we know. Indeed we must understand form, phrase, melody, harmony, texture, rhythm and meter, dynamics and articulation, our personal connection to the music, why it moves us, the composers' intentions etc.. And through our exploration of these musical matters, we hopefully will begin to understand how all these different aspects of the music relate to and influence one another. Understanding this interdependence is crucial to our being able to hear music unfold as it needs to. When we are alone on stage to perform, all we are left with is what we can hear. All the work and analysis that leads up to that moment, culminates in an aural conception of musical sound, an interpretation of music.

On the face of it, to consider all the things I speak of from the beginning of our learning does sound complicated, a lot to consider. But it is my contention, and my experience, that the more we look at music in this comprehensive, conceptual way from the beginning, the more apparent these relationships I speak of become. I am also suggesting to you, that this is a quicker, easier, more time efficient way to learn. It is a more wholistic way of learning, and because of that, how different aspects of the music relate to and influence one another are *always* part of the picture. We're not waiting until the end of the process to figure out how it all fits together. We are building from the beginning a more comprehensive, informed way of hearing the music, and as a result, the amount of unlearning we would otherwise have to do, is minimized. Our conception will evolve as we learn more and more about the music. Our hearing of the music will shift and change accordingly. Under these circumstances, *memorization becomes part of the process* and not something we have to do at the end of it, as if it were some kind of extra step. We should experience memorization as a natural result of our learning process, something connected to it, and not separate from it.

Thoughts

Always prepare as well as possible.........that's what professionals do.....

It's about ownership.....we don't want to lease a great composition we love, we want to own it. There's pride in ownership, not so much in leasing........be an owner.

All that we come to know and understand about music, all the theory, all the studying and practicing, our ability to play an instrument or sing with our voice, our musical philosophy and conception, must all get married to each other. Everything we are, musically and otherwise, must be integrated into one voice, our voice, into how we hear music. No part of our musical understanding should stand alone or be separate from any other part.......no secrets, only sharing.........everything needs to work together all the time..............

Music, like life, is about relationships............we have to always be on the lookout for musical relationships......

within a composition........... between styles............
with the other players and instruments we're playing
with.............as pianists between our right hand and
our left hand........................*no note stands alone, the
magic is in the relationships between them all..................
Aristotle believed man to be a social creature who finds
meaning in life in his/her relationship to other people. Music
is no different, individual notes, phrases, harmonies, rhythms,
compositional sections, musical sounds of any kind, all find
their meaning in each other.*

Don't avoid the obvious..........trust what you hear, what
you want to say...............be committed to it.........
and say it with conviction...........

Often developing improvisors seem to always be on the
search for a new idea. They often play enough ideas in
four bars to last a lifetime. It seems they think it is some-
how illegal to repeat something they have previously
played.

The task is to learn to work with one idea, the first one
that you play. We must learn to develop ideas, motives,
and trust that new ideas will emerge from that endeavor.

Speaking of developing ideas, I've been working with
some students on Wynton Kelly's solo on *"Freddie The
Freeloader"* from the legendary Miles Davis recording

"Kind Of Blue". Besides being part of what is arguably the greatest jazz recording of all time, it's as great an example as we could have of question and answer phrasing. The conversation couldn't be more clear. It's a great solo for all instrumentalists and vocalists as well to study.

On Teaching

There is no one size fits all. That is one of the challenges and joys of teaching. We have to find multiple ways to problem solve, multiple ways of expressing the same basic idea. Hopefully, that results in us having a variety of ways to affect change in our students. Perhaps that's why teachers often say "we learn more from our students than they from us".

I find something pure in the learning environment. A student or a group of students who want to learn, in a room with a teacher who wants to help them do just that. Learning and discovering are beautiful things to witness and be a part of. It doesn't matter if our role as teachers in a learning moment is big or small, whether we're just bearing witness to a student's discovery or we are more directly involved in the process. The learning process needs different things from us at different times, ranging from being very direct in our influence to being quite indirect. We have to know when to stay out of the way, when to challenge, when to ask questions, and when to provide answers.

Perhaps most importantly we have to understand that learning is a process, and it doesn't travel in a straight line.........doesn't always go according to plan or follow a logical order or go at the same speed, even for the same student..............each student's journey is different..........it goes in fits and starts.........fast then slow............seemingly long plateaus and then an unexpected jump to a new level........... two steps forward, one step back.............students do not always "connect the dots" or see musical relationships............. or think conceptually.........or see the "big picture", the forest instead of just the trees.............. sometimes we get too caught up in the trees, the details of music, and don't pay enough attention to broader musical concepts and understandings...... and sometimes we forget that we can be musical from the beginning................we don't have to wait until we "know all the notes" to be musical.........if we do, it's probably too late............. pitch, while extremely important, is just a part of the big musical picture.............and notes alone do not make music, any more than a pile of bricks makes a house...............we need to have a plan, know how and where to put those bricks.........which are part of the foundation which are decorative.............how do they fit into a phrase.............how does volume and touch and articulation affect them............I need a concept of the whole in order to know what to do with all those notes...........absent that, I just have a pile of bricks.............and that concept of the whole, or gestalt, needs to be considered from the beginning........... the first time we set our eyes on a musical composition, our priority is to come to an understanding of the whole...........that understanding will shift and change as we place more details inside of it.............our conception will evolve.............but we must start from the perspective of the whole, no matter how simplistic our initial gestalt might be...........we need a place for all the details.............we need a sense of where we are going and what we are trying to say.............it's hard to take a step or utter a coherent thought otherwise.................so in addition to teaching how to play a specific instrument, *we need to teach about music* and musicianship, about harmony and theory and form....... how to analyze and understand a piece of music......... come to some understanding of what the music at hand is about, what it might be trying to say.........what are the composers intentions......... what is it for us and how do we use all of our musical tools and concepts to express and communicate musically.......... *we need to teach a process*........a process of learning about and internalizing the music that moves us to become musicians and artists.

Chord Scales

I think perhaps it's time we rethink our educational emphasis on teaching chord scales. Let me say immediately that the teaching and learning of chord scales is an essential part of our theoretical musical education. As musical improvisors, it's simply part of what we need to know. That being said, we must provide a musical context for them.

Students too often seem to be under the impression that if they just play notes that are in what is deemed to be a good scale choice for a particular harmony, they're "good", forward moving music will result. But what happens much too often is vertical music, music that goes nowhere. The musical context is missing, and as a result we get vertical, station to station playing, chord to chord playing, or perhaps better said, one chord at a time playing, absent relationship to what came before or to what comes next. We get a pile of bricks, and a pile of bricks does not a house make. They need a plan, a relationship one to the other.

So what is the musical context I speak of? Well to start, it is specific to the tune being played, its melody and harmony, its tempo, meter and rhythms, its lyrics if it's a song. In short, it is everything you can think of that makes up the composition in question, including and importantly

its musical style. Even though we see similar chord pro-
gressions, similar rhythms and meters and tempos, similar
textures in different compositions, we must approach every piece of music we undertake to understand and play,
with a search for its uniqueness. It's not just a ballad, it is
this ballad, it's not just another I - vi - ii - V progression,
it's the one that is happening in this tune. Music is not
chords and slashes. I repeat, music is not chord symbols
and slashes. Chord symbols and slashes are simply chord
symbols and slashes, musical shorthand, nothing more...
...........a kind of notation.

Another problem that exists with chord scale centric
learning, is students tend to fall into a one scale per chord
approach..........that's it. I see this chord I play this scale
and this scale only. This is the complete antithesis to horizontal hearing, in fact I'll go so far as to say this isn't hearing at all, it's thinking, i.e. trying to think your way through
a piece instead of hearing your way through it. If we want
to truly hear our way through music, then hearing relationships is essential, and unavoidable. As I spoke of before, the relationship of pitch to pitch, individual pitch to
a harmony, harmony to harmony, tempo to meter, meter
to pulse, rhythm to pitch, rhythm to meter.........none
of these musical concepts happen in a vacuum, but they
happen in relationship to each other. It's all mixed up
together into a wonderful stew. Therein lies the magic,
the music, the energy, the forward movement. It's all in

these relationships and our understanding of them, and our relationship to them. That's where our voices are to be found, inside that musical stew.

Final Thoughts

I have been an improvising musician all of my life, and I have always aspired to be a jazz musician. Then I ended up at the University of Colorado in Boulder, Colorado and I met my teacher and mentor Dr. Guy Duckworth, and I learned about music. The style was the traditional piano literature from Bach to Barber, but we learned about music. The traditional literature just happened to be the vehicle for that learning.

Every style of music has its' idiosyncratic harmonic, rhythmic and melodic vocabulary. Every style of music has certain kinds of compositional forms that are unique to it or certainly prevalent within it. It is important, indeed imperative for us to understand as many genres of music as we possibly can, and in our chosen mode of musical expression, we must understand every aspect of its vocabulary completely.

That being said, I wonder if we can become too concerned with musical style? I wonder if being too "style

- centric" limits us, or hinders our development in some ways? And if we all adhere too religiously to stylistic norms, can musics evolve sufficiently?

I wonder these things as a jazz musician, as an improvising musician. But I also wonder about the impact of the above mentioned questions for all musicians playing all kinds of music, whether it be improvisational in nature or not. Do we want to limit the way we hear musical relationships? The way we hear a turn of phrase? The way we respond to a cadence? The way we feel time, meter and rhythm? The way we hear an improvisation or a written work unfold?

For me I think in the end, music has to win, has to come first. When we are there on stage alone with our instrument, with our voice, in the moment of performance, of musical expression, I think our prime objective has to be to make music, to express musically, and towards that end, to do the things that the music needs us to do. Let style be your vehicle, but *let music be the one you love.*

Gratitude

*Thank you to my teachers and my students and
all of the extraordinary musicians who have been
generous in sharing their knowledge and their
time with me, I am eternally grateful to you all.*

Special acknowledgements:

*Dr. Guy Duckworth, Dean Wesson, Ed Lucci,
Jimmy & Stacey Rowles, Tom Garvin, Alan
Broadbent, Richie Bierach, Putter Smith, Eric
Von Essen, Rich Falco, Larry Koonse*

*And thank you to all those who came before us,
who through their dedication and commitment
to musical expression, set artistic examples
for us all to follow and be inspired by.*